Look out for a
FREE MASK
Inside this Annual!

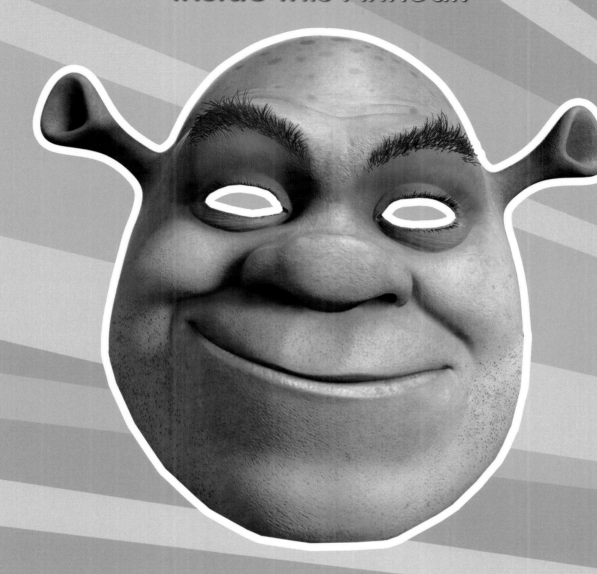

You Will Need:

- Thin elastic, wool or string
- Scissors
- Sticky Tape

Instructions:

1. Pull out the perforated mask page.
2. Pop out the mask.
3. Cut enough elastic/wool/string to fit around the back of your head.
4. Attach to the back of the mask with some sticky tape.
5. Have fun with your new mask!

SCISSORS ARE SHARP! ASK AN ADULT FOR HELP BEFORE USING.

CONTENTS

Pedigree®

Published 2013. Pedigree Books Limited, Beech Hill House,
Walnut Gardens, Exeter, Devon EX4 4DH.
www.pedigreebooks.com – books@pedigreegroup.co.uk
The Pedigree trademark, email and website addresses, are the
sole and exclusive properties of Pedigree
Group Limited, used under licence in this publication.

© 2013 DreamWorks Animation L.L.C.

DREAMWORKS
ANIMATION SKG

WELCOME

You're just in time! Inside you'll visit places that are Far Far Away...

Like Madagascar!

Or Ancient China!

And the Isle of Berk, where dragons fly through the sky!

So join us right here for the biggest party around! And maybe some karaoke too!

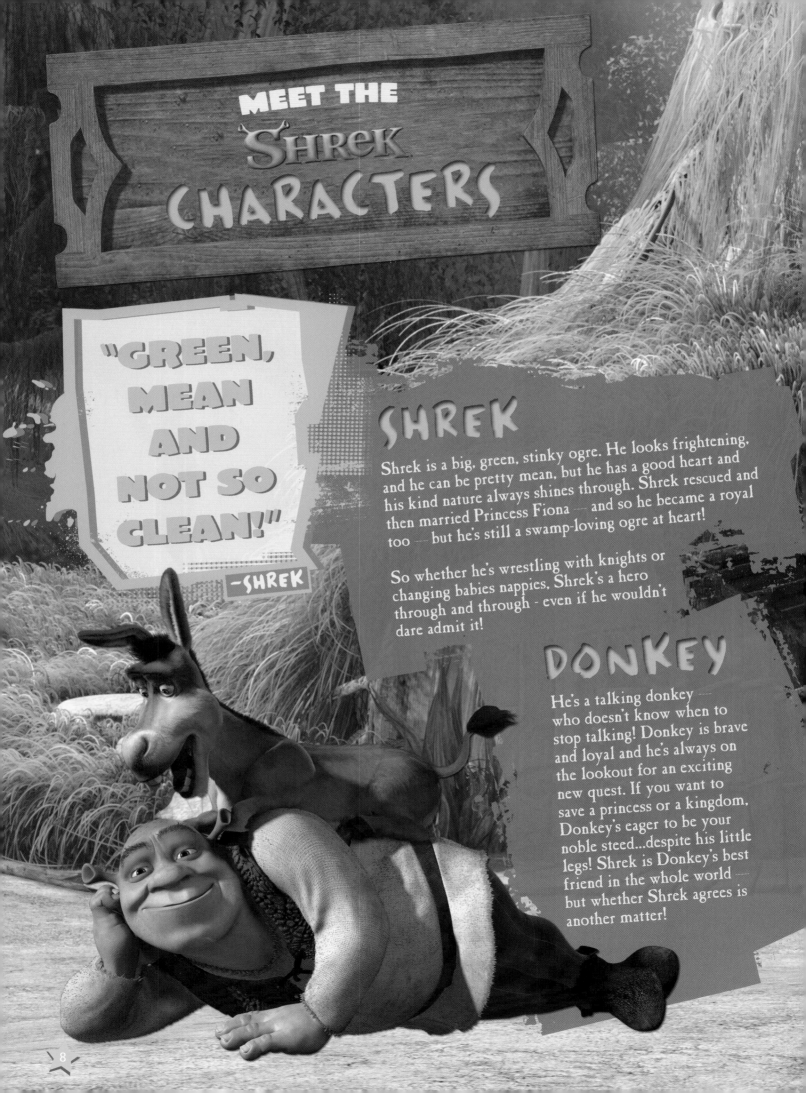

MEET THE
Shrek
CHARACTERS

"GREEN, MEAN AND NOT SO CLEAN!"

— SHREK

SHREK

Shrek is a big, green, stinky ogre. He looks frightening, and he can be pretty mean, but he has a good heart and his kind nature always shines through. Shrek rescued and then married Princess Fiona — and so he became a royal too — but he's still a swamp-loving ogre at heart!

So whether he's wrestling with knights or changing babies nappies, Shrek's a hero through and through - even if he wouldn't dare admit it!

DONKEY

He's a talking donkey — who doesn't know when to stop talking! Donkey is brave and loyal and he's always on the lookout for an exciting new quest. If you want to save a princess or a kingdom, Donkey's eager to be your noble steed...despite his little legs! Shrek is Donkey's best friend in the whole world — but whether Shrek agrees is another matter!

PRINCESS FIONA

Born a beautiful royal princess, Fiona was cursed by an evil spell — which happens a lot in the land of Far Far Away — to spend half her life as a fearsome-looking ogre until "true-loves kiss" released her. Fiona didn't expect that kiss to come from Shrek, nor that it would lock her in the form of an ogre forever! And would you believe — she's never been happier!

Fiona married Shrek and together they're sure that each day ends happily ever after — if only their kids would go to bed when they're told to!

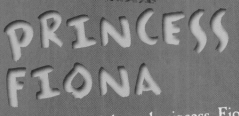

"THE POSITION OF ANNOYING TALKING ANIMAL HAS ALREADY BEEN TAKEN!"

—DONKEY

PUSS IN BOOTS

Claws, agility and a wicked line in smack-talk, Puss In Boots is the legendary ogre-slayer who ended up befriending Shrek. He's a master with a sword and has supreme fighting skills, but his greatest weapon is how cute he can look when he needs to.

Puss is always happy to join Shrek on a heroic adventure but, according to Donkey, he may just be one sidekick too many in Shrek's life!

DRAGON

Able to breathe fire, fly and destroy walls with a flick of her tail, Dragon made for an excellent guard of Princess Fiona's prison. That is, until the day Donkey melted the one thing Dragon's flaming breath couldn't — her heart! Donkey married his sweetheart Dragon and, despite the difference in their sizes — he's waist high to Shrek, she's waist high to the nearest mountain! — the two have never been happier!

"BURP!"
—DRAGON

LORD FARQUAAD

Lord Farquaad was the nasty ruler of Duloc and he doesn't have a kind bone in his body. He hated fairytale creatures cluttering up his land, but he made a mistake in asking for Shrek's help in his plan to marry Princess Fiona to make himself King. Shrek saved the Princess and Lord Farquaad never got to become king — instead he was eaten by Dragon!

THE FAIRY GODMOTHER AND PRINCE CHARMING

The Fairy Godmother is in the business of granting wishes. And when we say "business", we mean it — she's got business cards, slick advertisements and she oversees a factory that makes the magical stuff to grant wishes. She's also the mother of Prince Charming and she nurses a bitter grudge against Shrek because he married Princess Fiona before her son had a chance to! The fact that Prince Charming's a bit of a dope who couldn't rescue the last chocolate in a chocolate box doesn't help!

11

Saving The
PRINCESS

Once upon a time in the fairy tale land of Duloc, an ogre called Shrek enjoyed a quiet, lonely life in his own private swamp. That was until the day that Lord Farquaad, the cruel ruler of the land, dumped every fairytale creature in Shrek's swamp with him. Before long, the swamp was very overcrowded!

With Donkey guiding the way, Shrek went to see Lord Farquaad. Shrek agreed to save Princess Fiona from imprisonment in Dragon's Keep if Lord Farquaad would let him have his swamp back. Lord Farquaad agreed because he wanted to be king — and to do that he needed to marry a princess!

Neither Lord Farquaad nor Shrek knew that the beautiful Princess Fiona had been cursed by an evil spell to spend her nights as a hideous ogre, and that the only way to lift the curse was with "true love's kiss".

Shrek saved Princess Fiona from imprisonment, while Donkey sweet talked the guard dragon. On the journey home, Shrek and Fiona seemed to get along very well — could they be falling in love?

Once they were back in Duloc, Princess Fiona miserably agreed to marry Lord Farquaad, hoping that

it would free her from her terrible curse. But at the last moment, Shrek crashed the wedding and declared his love for Fiona, planting "true love's kiss" and lifting the curse. But when the curse was lifted, Fiona found she was no longer a beautiful princess — she was now a green ogre all of the time!

Lord Farquaad was overthrown and eaten by the dragon — who was now dating Donkey — while Shrek married Princess Fiona. Together Shrek and Fiona set off for new adventures as the greenest, scaliest, smelliest pair of newlyweds that the fairytale lands had ever seen!

Saving The
KINGDOM!

Of course, no one said that marrying a royal princess was easy!

Shrek was out of his depth when he met with Princess Fionas snooty human parents in the land of Far Far Away, so he stole a magic potion from the Fairy Godmother to grant his wish to fit in with them. The wish transformed Shrek into a human — only to find that Fiona no longer recognised him! Meanwhile, the scheming Fairy Godmother was making her own plans — she wanted her son, Prince Charming (who was not charming at all!) to marry Princess Fiona and one day become king. So while the now-human Shrek was struggling to prove his identity, Prince Charming made his move on Princess Fiona. True love won the day however, and with the help of Donkey and Puss In Boots, Shrek and Fiona were reunited just in time to stop the Fairy Godmother's wicked plans... and Shrek was soon back to his old green self!

=LIVE HAPPILY EVER AFTER=

Ogre Again!

Shortly after that, Shrek found out that he was next in line to be king--a role he could not imagine! So, with Donkey's help, Shrek searched for the missing heir to the throne of Far Far Away. While Shrek was gone, Prince Charming tried to take over the kingdom with an army of fairytale Villain ——only to be stopped by Princess Fiona and her squadron of fairytale Princesses!

After he had saved the kingdom and neatly escaped becoming its king, Shrek started to miss his old days of being a mean and scary ogre. Foolishly, Shrek asked Rumpelstilkstin to use his magic

to get him his "roar" back —— but the plan backfired, and Shrek found himself in a mixed-up world where no one remembered all the good he had done. This time, Shrek had just 24 hours to put everything back the way it was — and make sure that he could stay Shrek forever!

Of course he did it — like a smelly burp, you can't keep a good ogre down!

MIXED-UP Wishes

The Fairy Godmother has mixed up her wishes. Can you work out who wished for what?

ATTACH ELASTIC
WITH TAPE HERE

ATTACH ELASTIC
WITH TAPE HERE

Wish 1:

"I wish I had a babysitter who was flame-proof."

This wish is from...

Wish 2:

"I wish my husband Shrek would stop walking mud into our swamp home."

This wish is from...

Wish 3:

"I wish my nose was shorter!"

This wish is from...

Wish 4:

"I wish I could have another exciting adventure where I can be the noble steed to my best friend."

This wish is from...

Wish 5:

"I wish I was taller so I could look down on my subjects."

This wish is from...

Wish 6:

"I wish I had some really colourful earwax to make a new candle for my wife Fiona."

This wish is from...

Wish 7:

"I wish I could have a nice bowl of creamy milk to drink!"

This wish is from...

Wish 8:

Now it's your turn!
What would you wish for?

I wish

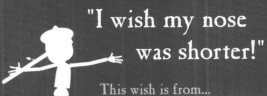

17

HOW TO BE A NOBLE STEED!

"NO HERO WORTH THE NAME WILL GO ON A QUEST WITHOUT THEIR NOBLE STEED. THERE AIN'T NOTHING BETTER THAN BEING A NOBLE STEED! HERE ARE MY TOP TIPS FOR BEING THE BEST OF THE BEST..."

TIP 1 · KEEPING FIT!

A noble steed needs to stay fit. There are a lot of monsters to run away from when you're on a quest! One time when I was out with Shrek we got attacked by enchanted trees who wouldn't "leaf" us alone!

Try jumping up and down on the spot five times to make sure you're fit for the job! And no cheating — noble steeds never tell lies!

TIP 2 · KEEPING COOL!

A noble steed stays cool under pressure. Without me, Shrek would have been caught in the rain without an umbrella more than once! And trust me, "soggy" is no look for a hero when he's rescuing a pretty princess.

SO NOW IT'S YOUR TURN!

There were eight different people at the start of the Shrek pages in this book — how many can you remember? No peeking until you've got as many as you can think of!

TIP 3 · MOVING QUICK!

A noble steed is always ready for action! I am so ready for action that sometimes I'm on a quest with Shrek and he doesn't even know that we're on a quest!

Try hopping on one foot ten times and then hopping on the other ten times to prove you're quick enough for the job!

TIP 4: STAYING ALERT!

A noble steed has to pay attention! These two pictures may look the same but they're not!

CAN YOU SPOT ALL SIX DIFFEENCES?

LOOKING IN THE
Magic Mirror

Donkey's looking into the Magic Mirror.
Help him out by colouring the things he sees!

"Magic Mirror,
tall and clever,
Show me
who'll be
my best
friend forever?"

—DONKEY

SHREK'S FAIRYTALE
HOROSCOPES

Once Upon a Time

TRUE LOVE'S First Kiss

ARIES

Something's cooking today, Aries — you're looking good enough to eat!

GEMINI

You can be a little short-tempered, so why not try to be the bigger man.

CANCER

My, what big plans you have today! By the afternoon, you'll be grinning from ear to ear!

TAURUS

Stop making up stories and try to keep your big nose out of other people's business today.

LEO

Thumbs up, Leo — you always have your finger on the pulse! Give yourself a big hand.

VIRGO

You have a busy day ahead, so make sure you get plenty of rest. Why not take an afternoon nap?

LIBRA

Everything's pointing in the right direction for you today. Just make sure you stay on target!

SAGITTARIUS

You may be being kept in the dark so, if you're feeling lost, trust your friends to lead the way!

CAPRICORN

You have a magical day ahead where you'll get everything you wish for.

SCORPIO

You'll be in a reflective mood today, but you may find your attention wandering.

PISCES

You'll receive an invitation to a very special ball — but remember not to stay too late!

Live Happily Ever After

AQUARIUS

You like things to be just right, but try putting yourself in someone else's shoes (or chair or bed) today and maybe you'll cool down (just like your porridge).

SHREK

OGRES HAVE LAYERS

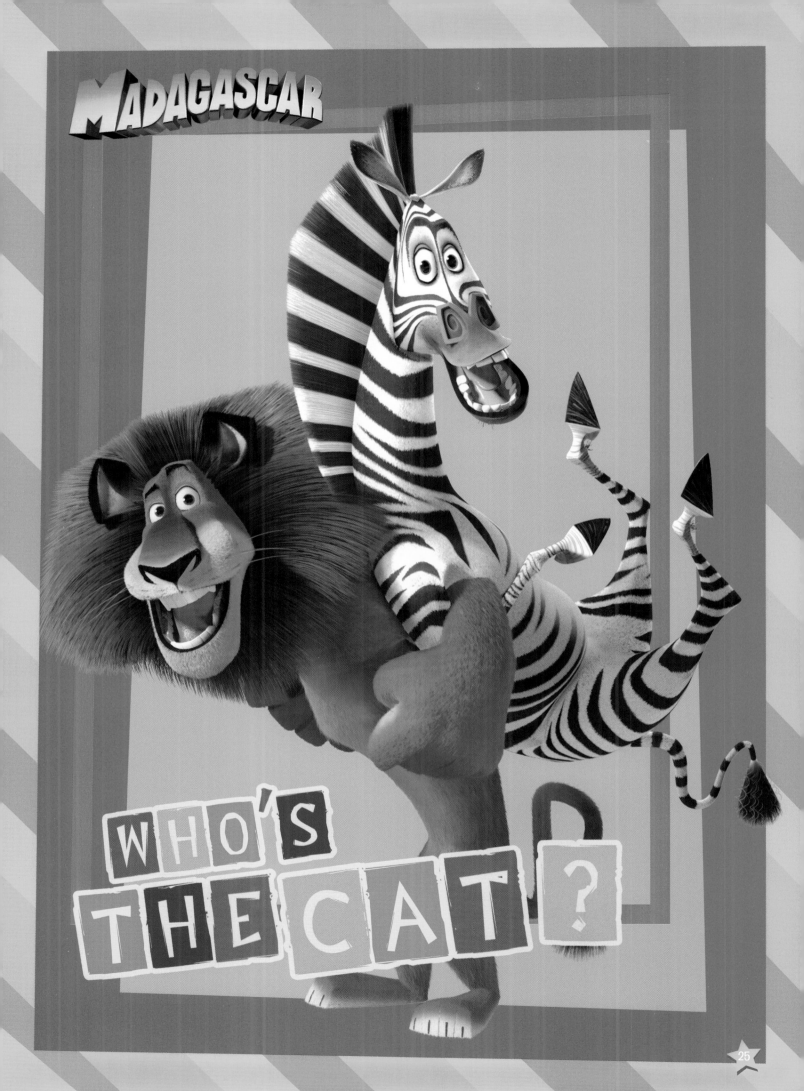

Meet the MADAGASCAR CHARACTERS

ALEX

Alex the lion used to be the star of the New York City Zoo, until he was stranded on the island of Madagascar. He's best friends with Marty and they're always trying to better each other!

MARTY

Marty is a zebra who loves to dream and longs to get back to his roots. Right now he doesn't even know if he's black with white stripes or white with black stripes!

"WAS THIS SPOT ON MY NECK ALWAYS THERE?"

-Melman

MELMAN

Melman is a giraffe who worries about every illness under the sun. No one knows if Melman is really sick or not — but he's clever and he's always loyal to his friends.

GLORIA

Gloria's a smart, sassy hippo who doesn't take any nonsense from anyone! She loved having her own swimming pool in the New York Zoo, but no matter where she goes, she always manages to stay happy.

THE PENGUINS

These four fellows may look cute and cuddly, but that's just part of their act. Led by Skipper, the Penguins are always working on new plans with military precision.

RICO

In charge of weapons, he loves blowing things up!

KOWALSKI

Makes the plans and reads the maps!

PRIVATE

The heart of this Penguin team.

"IT'S NOTHING PERSONAL, IT'S JUST THAT WE'RE BETTER THAN YOU!" *-King Julien*

KING JULIEN

This king of the Lemurs loves to party! King Julien loves bossing people around. He's sure that he's better than everyone else — and he doesn't hesitate to remind them.

MAURICE AND MORT

Maurice is an aye-aye who works as King Julien's faithful assistant. And boy, does he work hard! Maurice is loyal and puts up with the king's quirks — even when he's made the butt of King Julien's jokes.

Mort is a mouse lemur who's always bouncy and happy. King Julien thinks he's so cute it's annoying.

FROM ZOO TO SOME PLACE NEW!

On his tenth birthday, Marty wondered whether he wanted to live in the New York Zoo for the rest of his life. He had great friends there - Alex, Gloria and Melman - but the Penguins had told him that animals belonged in "the wild" and they were working on a plan to escape.

That evening, Marty snuck out of the zoo, but he was soon caught. However, the animal lovers decided to send all the animals back to their natural homes on a ship bound for a wildlife Preserve in Africa, where they hoped they would be happier.

The wily Penguins commandeered the ship and, when they changed course, Marty, Alex, Gloria and Melman tumbled from the deck and into the sea!

The four friends washed ashore on the strange island of Madagascar where they were befriended by the eccentric King Julien, ruler of the crazy Lemurs. Lemurs loved to party, but their fun

was always being ruined by the foosa - nasty, cat-like creatures who wanted to eat them. After seeing Alex frighten the foosa away, King Julien realised that he would be a perfect bodyguard - and all the king needed to do was treat these "New York Giants" well.

However, Alex was struggling to find anything to eat on the island. Back in the zoo, he had been fed steak every day, but out here in the wild he had become so hungry he even dreamed about eating his best friend Marty!

Alex was so scared that he might hurt Marty that he hid himself away in the heart of foosa territory.

Just then, the Penguins returned with the ship, offering everyone a chance to sail home to New York. Marty refused to leave the island without Alex but when he went to talk some sense into him he became surrounded by the nasty foosa! Melman, Gloria and the Penguins tried to help but they all were soon surrounded and outnumbered.

Seeing his friends in trouble made Alex realise how much they meant to him. Alex chased the foosa away for good.

By now, Alex was really hungry! But the Penguins had the perfect solution - they made him a fish dinner that tasted even better than steak! Now he would never think about eating his friends again!

GOING HOME
OR GETTING LOST?

The Wild can be a pretty scary place, but getting back to New York proved more difficult than the friends imagined. With no fuel left in the ship, the friends tried several different ways to escape Madagascar.

A plane trip ended with a crash landing that dumped the friends in the African wildlife preserve where Alex's family lived. Alex, Marty, Gloria and Melman found new groups of friends there - animals of their own kind who were delighted to have these newcomers join them. But before long, problems began to show and the friends realised they did not really fit in the wild.

CIRCUS ACT

Alex, Marty, Gloria and Melman tried another way home to New York, but they became sidetracked into Europe. While there, the zoo animals attracted the attention of the local "Animal Control" people and had to find a way to travel without drawing too much attention to themselves.

But how can a lion, a zebra, a hippo, a giraffe, four penguins, two monkeys and three lemurs travel across Europe without being noticed? They signed up as members of a travelling circus, and managed to turn its fortunes around!

The friends loved the circus and realised that maybe it was even better than being in the New York Zoo!

Where the zoo gang will end up next is anyone's guess! But you can bet it will be somewhere wild!

Melman's MESSED-UP MEMORY QUIZ

"OH NO, I MUST BE VERY UNWELL! I CAN'T REMEMBER ANYTHING! CAN YOU HELP REMIND ME OF THESE FACTS? I'M SURE THEY MUST BE IMPORTANT!"

1 Which zoo does Melman, Alex, Gloria and Marty come from?

2 How old was Marty when his friends celebrated his birthday in the zoo?

3 What type of animal is Gloria?

4 How many Penguins are there in the zoo team?

5 Where was the ship headed when Melman and his friends tumbled off the deck?

6 Who is the king of the Lemurs?

7 What animals are the Lemurs most afraid of on the island of Madagascar?

8 What food do the Penguins give to Alex?

ALEX VS

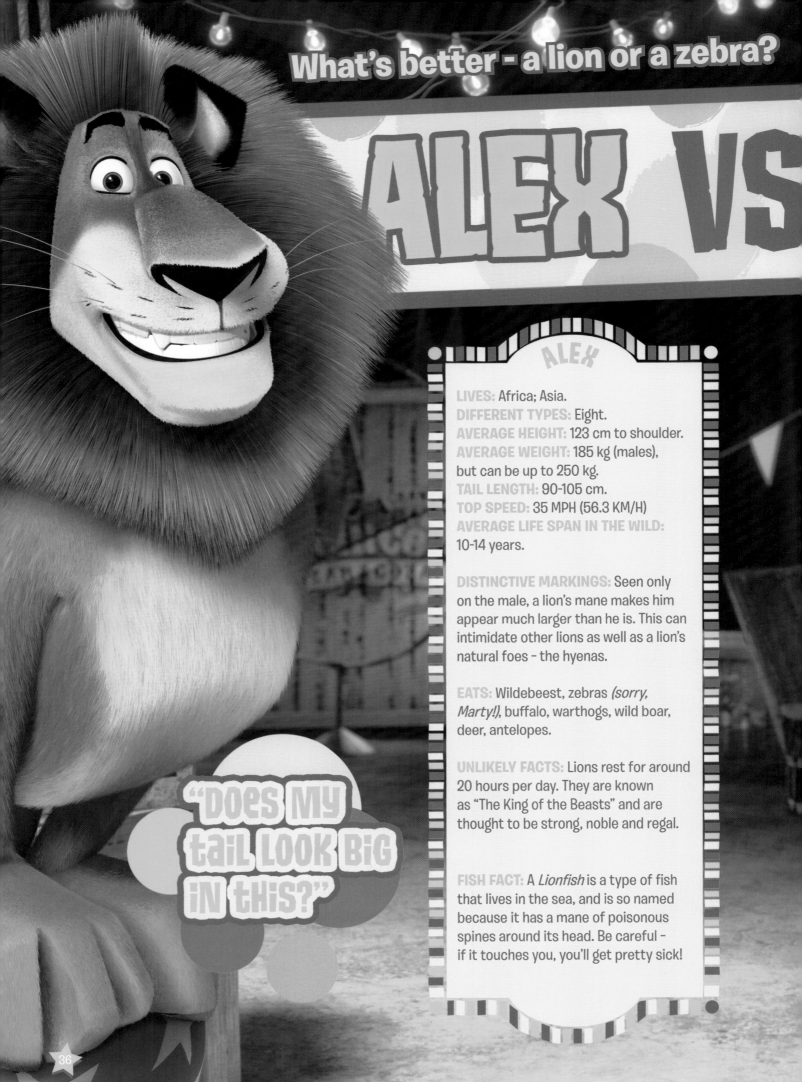

ALEX

LIVES: Africa; Asia.
DIFFERENT TYPES: Eight.
AVERAGE HEIGHT: 123 cm to shoulder.
AVERAGE WEIGHT: 185 kg (males), but can be up to 250 kg.
TAIL LENGTH: 90-105 cm.
TOP SPEED: 35 MPH (56.3 KM/H)
AVERAGE LIFE SPAN IN THE WILD: 10-14 years.

DISTINCTIVE MARKINGS: Seen only on the male, a lion's mane makes him appear much larger than he is. This can intimidate other lions as well as a lion's natural foes - the hyenas.

EATS: Wildebeest, zebras *(sorry, Marty!)*, buffalo, warthogs, wild boar, deer, antelopes.

UNLIKELY FACTS: Lions rest for around 20 hours per day. They are known as "The King of the Beasts" and are thought to be strong, noble and regal.

FISH FACT: A *Lionfish* is a type of fish that lives in the sea, and is so named because it has a mane of poisonous spines around its head. Be careful - if it touches you, you'll get pretty sick!

"DOES MY TAIL LOOK BIG IN THIS?"

MARTY

MARTY

LIVES: Africa.
DIFFERENT TYPES: Three.
AVERAGE HEIGHT: 130 cm to shoulder.
AVERAGE WEIGHT: 350 kg.
TAIL LENGTH: 50 cm.
TOP SPEED: 40 MPH (64.4 KM/H).
AVERAGE LIFE SPAN IN THE WILD: 25 years.

DISTINCTIVE MARKINGS:
Black and white stripes which act as camouflage in long grass and may also confuse predators.

EATS: Mostly grass, but also shrubs, herbs, twigs, leaves and bark.

UNLIKELY FACTS:
Zebras have excellent eyesight, hearing, smell and taste.

FISH FACT: The *Zebrafish* is a blue-and-white striped minnow that lives in the streams of Asia. In 2008, scientists developed a new strain of Zebrafish called "Casper" that was completely see-through!

"WHEN A ZEBRA'S IN THE ZONE, LEAVE HIM ALONE!"

The GREAT ESCAPE

"Face it, boys – a zoo is no place for a penguin. We need to get out there in the wild – that's where all the action is! So let's see your plans for getting out!"

RICO'S PLAN: GETTING JUMPY!
Leave the zoo on a kangaroo! The kangaroo jumps the wall, and we just hang on for a ride!

TOO DANGEROUS, WE MIGHT GET TRAVEL SICK.

- SKIPPER

KOWALSKI'S PLAN: BADDA-BING, BADDA-ZOOM!!
Dig a tunnel using discarded plastic spoons.

GOOD JOB, KOWALSKI, BUT MAKE SURE WE HAVE ENOUGH SPOONS!

- SKIPPER

PRIVATE'S PLAN: SURF'S UP!
Run across the backs of the turtles to the zoo wall and then leap over.

COULD WORK, PRIVATE! BUT WON'T THOSE TURTLES BE SLIPPERY?

- SKIPPER

YOUR PLAN:

"Now it's your turn, recruit. How would you escape this penguin prison? Include a picture, too, showing how your plan works."

MARINE INTELLIGENCE

TIME TO MIGRATE

SOUTH POLE OR BUST

PENGUIN
HABITAT

FREEDOM!!!

You've done this unit proud,
soldier, but here comes the
real test. Find your way out
of the zoo on this map?

IMPEACH Skipper

A good soldier can only trust his own team. See if you can find them, and anyone else, in this picture!

Meet the KUNG FU PANDA™ CHARACTERS

PO

Though he works in his father's noodle restaurant, Po the panda dreams of being a respected kung fu warrior like his heroes, the Furious Five. When he is chosen to become the legendary Dragon Warrior, Po thinks his dream has come true – but he soon discovers being a kung fu master isn't as easy as he imagined.

THIS KUNG FU STUFF IS HARD WORK

– PO

MASTER SHIFU

A highly respected kung fu master, this red panda is the instructor at the temple. Master Shifu is highly disciplined – he trained the Furious Five and their mortal enemy, Tai Lung. But he's never had a student like Po before, and he doubts that he'll ever get this big panda into shape!

MASTER OOGWAY

A wise and ancient tortoise, Master Oogway is the spiritual leader of the Valley of Peace. He is hundreds of years old, and very learned. Despite the objections of Master Shifu, Master Oogway has no doubt that fate has delivered the Dragon Warrior to the temple when Po is accidentally chosen for training.

THE FURIOUS FIVE

The most brilliant kung fu warriors in all of China, the Furious Five's adventures are already the stuff of legend.

MONKEY

Playful and energetic.

CRANE

Calm and observant.

TIGRESS

Strong and fearless.

VIPER

Charming and deadly.

MANTIS

Tiny and lethal.

TAI LUNG

Trained in the art of kung fu by Master Shifu, this powerful snow leopard could be the greatest martial artist in all of China. But Tai Lung is selfish and jealous, and he craves the power of the Dragon Scroll. Tai Lung breaks free from prison to claim the legendary Scroll – and fulfil his cruel destiny.

YOU CAN'T DEFEAT ME! YOU... YOU'RE JUST A BIG... FAT... PANDA!

– TAI LUNG

MR PING

This cheerful goose is Po's father and he runs the local noodle restaurant, just like his father and grandfather before him. He loves his son, Po, but he doubts that he'll ever make a good noodle seller when he spends so much time daydreaming.

IT SMELLS LIKE TOFU!

USING HIS NOODLE

Po the panda seemed an unlikely choice when he was selected to learn kung fu and become the legendary Dragon Warrior. Po was overweight, he couldn't fight and he got beaten up by the punch bag! In fact, Po was so hopeless, that back when he had worked in his father's noodle shop, his dad had never shared his secret recipe for his "special noodle soup".

Yet Po had been selected by wise Master Oogway for training in the temple of the Valley of Peace beside his heroes – the legendary Furious Five – under their brilliant teacher, Master Shifu. But no matter how hard he tried, all Po was really good at was cooking and eating!

Master Shifu pleaded with Master Oogway to reconsider his choice – the temple had waited a thousand years to train the Dragon Warrior, surely one of the Furious Five was better suited? But Oogway saw great courage in Po and he trusted that fate had brought the perfect student.

Then Oogway died and his spirit became one with nature. Shifu agreed to honour his master's final request and train Po, but he would have to do so quickly - Oogway had foreseen the arrival of Tai Lung, a selfish kung fu warrior who would stop at nothing to steal the power of the Dragon Scroll and become Dragon Warrior himself. Tai Lung had recently escaped a high security prison designed just for him, and defeated the Furious Five on his journey to the temple to steal the scroll.

Shifu tricked Po into combat training by promising him food. If Po wanted to eat, he would have to fight the great kung fu master! It was the perfect motivation!

Po found himself performing combat moves that he thought he'd never do, and he was finally proven the right choice to become Dragon Warrior.

THE DRAGON SCROLL
REVEALED!

owever, there was one final twist. When Po looked at the Dragon Scroll - *it didn't say anything!* The scroll was supposed to give him limitless powers, but its mirrored surface was blank. Without the promised powers, what could Po do to stop Tai Lung?

Just then, the Furious Five returned, having failed in their mission to stop Tai Lung, and the decision was made to evacuate the village. Master Shifu would stay at the temple to fight Tai Lung - and even though he could not win, he hoped to give everyone enough time to leave the village, including Po.

Po went sadly back to his father's noodle shop to help pack everything away. He had failed and that failure would cost everyone their home. But he was still a hero in his father's eyes, because he had tried. His father told Po that he was ready now to share his secret recipe for "special noodle soup" with him. "The secret ingredient is... nothing!" he revealed. "To make something special you just have to believe it is special."

Po could not believe what he was hearing. He looked back at the legendary Dragon Scroll and saw his face reflected on its golden surface, and realised that the thing that made him the Dragon Warrior - that made him special - was that he believed in himself.

Tai Lung had defeated Shifu by the time Po returned to defend the temple. Tai Lung dismissed Po as a fat panda, so he was surprised when Po showed him the greatest kung fu moves he would ever see! Their battle raged across the village, until finally Tai Lung grabbed the Dragon Scroll. But he did not understand what he saw there - why was the scroll blank? That was the final defeat for Tai Lung, distracting and confusing him so that Po could use Master Shifu's special move to defeat him. Po was hailed as a hero!

Long live Po, the dragon warrior!

KUNG FU
FIREWORKS!

But peace did not remain for long. A new warrior, the evil Lord Shen, soon challenged Po and the Furious Five, armed with a spectacular new weapon. After killing a grand kung fu master called Thundering Rhino, Lord Shen attacked the temple with his new weapon - a devastatingly powerful cannon.

Brilliant fighting was not enough to defeat this villain. Finally Po drew on meditation techniques and his own inner calm to defeat Lord Shen.

MASTER SHIFU'S
SCROLL TEST

A great warrior must remember the things he or she is told. Show me that you are able to do this by answering these questions...

NUMBER 1
Q. Who is the chosen Dragon Warrior?

NUMBER 2
Q. What type of creature is Po's father, Mister Ping?

NUMBER 3
Q. Who is the smallest member of the Furious Five?

NUMBER 4
Q. Which member of the Furious Five has wings?

NUMBER 5
Q. What job does Po's dad do?

NUMBER 6
Q. What is the secret ingredient in Po's dad's special noodle soup?

NUMBER 7
Q. Which powerful, sacred object does Tai Lung hope to steal?

NUMBER 8
Q. What reward does Master Shifu use to train Po?

KUNG FU PANDA'S
BEST JOKES

What goes black, white, black, white, black, white, black, white...
A PANDA ROLLING DOWN A HILL!

What did the ghost panda say to scare Po?

"BAM-BOO!"

What's black and white and wears sunglasses?

A PANDA IN DISGUISE!

Did you hear what happened when Po's dad discovered him eating without any clothes on?

HE CAUGHT HIM IN THE NUDELES (NOODLES)!

What happens when Po can't decide what to eat?

HE'S BAMBOOZLED!

Why did Po like Master Shifu's feet?

BECAUSE HE ALWAYS GOT A KICK OUT OF THEM!

What's black and white and red all over?
A SUNBURNT PANDA!

What do you call a panda in the arctic?
LOST!

DO YOU DO KUNG FU?

Training to be the Dragon Warrior wasn't easy. Take a look at Po's diary and maybe you can help him out.

MONDAY

Another day, another noodle! I sure wish Dad would tell me what he puts in his special noodle soup — I'd like to know what it is I'm balancing when I carry all those dishes!

What secret ingredient would you add? (maybe some tomato ketchup or ice cream!)

I would add
....
....
....
....

TUESDAY

Met the Furious Five —
who are *awesome!*
They are a lot bigger in
real life than their action
figures...Except for Mantis
who is about the same.
Better make sure that
I remember their names by
writing them here.

1 ....

2 ....

3 ....

4 ....

5 ....

WEDNESDAY

Master Shifu sure knows
his kung fu! By the end of
our first training session
I was seeing stars!

Add some stars around
Po's head, and colour the
picture in.

THURSDAY

Training to be a kung fu master is really hungry work so I cooked up a great dinner for all my new friends!

What would you feed to the Furious Five?

....
....
....
....
....

FRIDAY

I learned to sit down, *kung fu style!* I am well on my way to being a Kung Fu Panda!

Colour in Po and Master Shifu and draw a picture of what Po is thinking about in the thought balloon – maybe it could be his dinner, the Dragon Scroll or one of the Furious Five!

BE SLOW TO EAT QUICK TO ACT

SATURDAY

AWESOME!
Met the crazy Tai Lung and busted some moves all over him! He went down like a plate of wet noodles.

SUNDAY

Help Po find his way around the noodle shop to deliver food to the hungry customers.

MEET THE
HOW TO TRAIN YOUR
DRAGON
CHARACTERS

Stoick
THE VAST

The brave chief of the Viking tribe on the Isle of Berk, Stoick is the greatest dragon slayer alive. He leads the charge when it comes to protecting his people from dragons, and he hopes to one day destroy the dragons' nest, home of all dragons.

Hiccup
HORRENDOUS HADDOCK III

Hiccup is the son of the brave chief Stoick and he tries to live up to his father's legendary reputation. However, Hiccup's small and not very strong and he's better at making things than killing them! Hiccup's gentle nature comes in handy when he finds a poor, wounded dragon!

Astrid
HOFFERSON

A beautiful and brave
girl who's training to be
a dragon slayer. Astrid is
quick and strong and she
shows no fear, even in the
face of the most dangerous
foe. Little wonder then that
all the Viking boys have
fallen in love with her –
but she's too busy learning
to slay dragons to notice!

Gobber
THE BELCH

The village blacksmith, Gobber trains the next
generation of warriors to fight dragons.
He's brave and knows every
dragon's weakness, but
even that couldn't save
him from losing a hand
and a foot in battle.

What sound does a
dragon's phone make?

IT "WINGS"!

Tuffnut Ruffnut
THORSTON   THORSTON

Bickering twin brother and sister, Ruffnut Thorston and Tuffnut Thorston are determined to prove which one of them is the best. But their competitive nature means they often get in one another's way – and fixing that may be a Tuffnut...or is it a Ruffnut...to crack!

How does a dragon weigh something?

By placing it on its scales!

Snotlout
JORGENSON

Snotlout is the ideal Viking – he's mean, he bullies and he can't wait to get into a fight! Snotlout fancies classmate Astrid and thinks Hiccup is nothing but a coward. But he has to change his tune when he sees the way that Hiccup controls the dragons!

Fishlegs
INGERMAN

Fishlegs knows a lot about dragons. He's read the books and memorised the stats. But when it comes to fighting one, he's still utterly clueless. To make things even worse, tubby Fishlegs isn't built for running away...well, not very fast, anyway!

Could You Slay A DRAGON?

Hiccup wanted to be a dragon slayer like his father Stoick, the brave chief of the tribe on the Isle of Berk. But Hiccup wasn't strong like his dad – all he was good at was helping the local blacksmith make swords and armour for the real warriors!

Hiccup used a huge catapult to strike an attacking Night Fury dragon from the sky during a dragon raid. The dragon was wounded, and when Hiccup saw how scared it was he realised that he could not kill it, no matter how fearsome it seemed. So he freed the Night Fury and let it fly away.

But the wounded Night Fury could not fly properly to escape the valley. Now Hiccup didn't know what to do.

Meanwhile, Chief Stoick announced his plan to find and destroy the dragons' nest to stop the dragons raiding his village ever again. Hiccup and the other kids would remain behind for Dragon Training and would learn to fight like their parents.

On the first day of training, Hiccup was terrified – he wasn't a dragon killer and he never would be! His classmates laughed at him, while his teacher, Gobber, despaired. Like all the other boys, Hiccup wished he could impress Astrid, the pretty girl in his class.

After class, Hiccup searched for the wounded Night Fury in the valley near the village. The wounded dragon was still there – it could not fly well enough to leave. Hiccup felt sorry for the dragon so he came back again and again to feed it. The Night Fury was timid at first but soon warmed to Hiccup. It even shared its half-eaten fish with him!

While Hiccup trained to slay dragons in his classes, he secretly befriended the Night Fury in his spare time. He even gave it a name – Toothless! Hiccup helped Toothless recover, and built Toothless an artificial tail rudder to help it fly again. Hiccup even used a saddle to fly on Toothless' back. Soon, the two friends were flying over the ocean together!

As Hiccup learned more about Toothless, he discovered ways to tame other dragons without actually hurting them.

TOP OF THE CLASS!

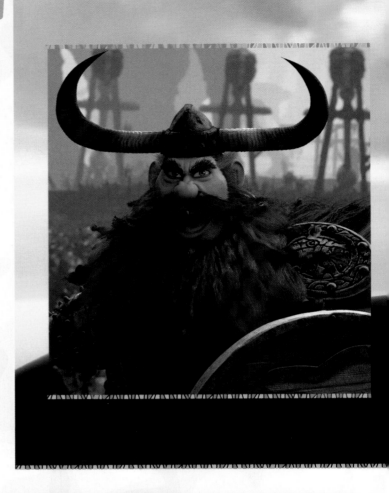

Hiccup became the star pupil in class. He never had to fight a dragon – he just used all the tricks he had learned from Toothless!

But classmate Astrid was suspicious. She followed Hiccup and discovered his pet dragon! Astrid couldn't believe it at first, but she soon became friends with Toothless – especially after the dragon let her fly on its back!

Hiccup was about to graduate top of his class when his father and the other warriors returned home. They had failed to find the dragons' nest.

Chief Stoic was overjoyed to learn that his son had excelled in Dragon Training and he could not wait to see the boy face the final challenge – an arena battle with a Monstrous Nightmare dragon. But Hiccup refused to hurt the dragon and he told the villagers there was another way – to befriend the dragons instead.

Stoick stopped the fight but the commotion sent the Monstrous Nightmare into a frenzy, and Hiccup was almost killed – until faithful Toothless came to rescue him! Now Hiccup's secret was revealed and he was in a lot of trouble!

Chief Stoick was very angry with his son but he realised he could use Toothless to help locate the dragons' nest. Hiccup was left at home while his dad and the Viking warriors sailed away to destroy the nest.

Hiccup knew that he could help, if only his father would listen. Hiccup pleaded with his fellow students to help him, and he showed each of them how to ride one of the captured dragons that they had trained with. Astrid believed in him – she knew that he had trained Toothless.

The kids flew to the dragons' nest just as the biggest dragon – a Red Death Dragon – destroyed

the Viking longboats. The Red Death Dragon was a colossal monster who seemed too large and powerful to stop!

While his classmates rode their dragons to help the struggling Viking warriors, Hiccup rode Toothless once more, battling with the Red Death Dragon herself. Both dragon and rider were almost consumed by the Red Death's fiery breath but they tricked the bigger dragon into an impossible dive that she could not pull out of. At last, the big dragon was dead.

Hiccup lost a leg in that battle. But he had gained a friend in Toothless and something more too – he had gained the respect of his father and all of the village. Now dragons and humans would work and live together!

Written in fire

1. Where does Hiccup work?

2. Who is Hiccup's father?

3. Where does Hiccup live?

4. What type of dragon is Toothless?

5. Who teaches the Dragon Training class?

6. Including Hiccup, how many students are there in the Dragon Training class?

7. What is the name of the pretty girl in Hiccup's class?

8. What food does Toothless share with Hiccup?

9. What type of dragon is the big dragon?

Know Your DRAGONS

NIGHT FURY

The unholy offspring of lightning and death itself. Never engage this dragon – hide and pray it does not find you!

Hiccup's tip: Night Furies are actually kind of shy. Just be gentle, dont make any sudden moves and try offering it some food.

GRONCKLE

Strong jawed with a vicious bite, the Gronckle has six shots of fiery breath to charcoal its victims, too. It's main weakness is its poor manoeuvrability when in an enclosed space.

Hiccup's tip: Tickle its nose with grass: get it right and the Gronckle will be putty in your hands!

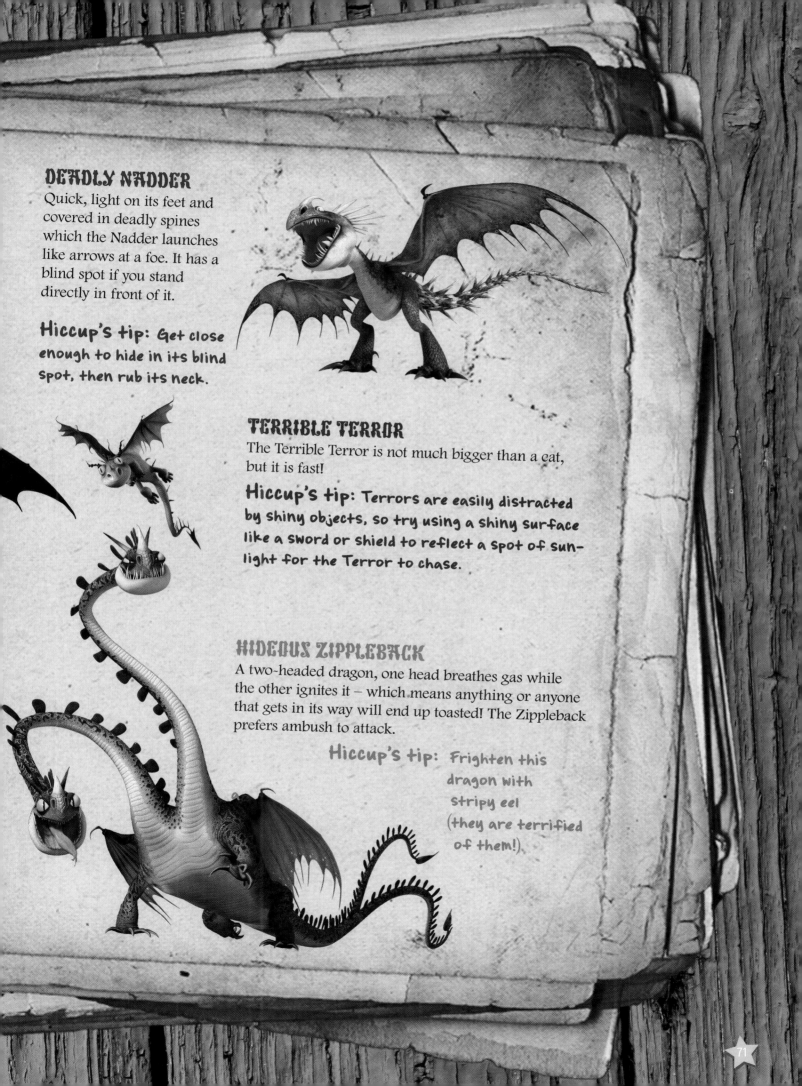

DEADLY NADDER

Quick, light on its feet and covered in deadly spines which the Nadder launches like arrows at a foe. It has a blind spot if you stand directly in front of it.

Hiccup's tip: Get close enough to hide in its blind spot, then rub its neck.

TERRIBLE TERROR

The Terrible Terror is not much bigger than a cat, but it is fast!

Hiccup's tip: Terrors are easily distracted by shiny objects, so try using a shiny surface like a sword or shield to reflect a spot of sunlight for the Terror to chase.

HIDEOUS ZIPPLEBACK

A two-headed dragon, one head breathes gas while the other ignites it – which means anything or anyone that gets in its way will end up toasted! The Zippleback prefers ambush to attack.

Hiccup's tip: Frighten this dragon with stripy eel (they are terrified of them!)

MONSTROUS NIGHTMARE

A large, fast-moving monster with fiery breath. Monstrous Nightmare is prone to set itself alight in combat, but its scales are flameproof so beware if you get in its way!

Hiccup's tip: No fast movements, just talk calmly and softly.

BONE KNAPPER

A mysterious dragon who wears discarded bones like armour. Very dangerous, do not approach.

Hiccup's tip: Tempt the Bone Knapper with a piece of bone and you may be able to befriend it.

RED DEATH DRAGON

Ruler of the dragon nest, the Red Death Dragon is a colossal monster. She has multiple eyes, can fly and is capable of breaking a longboat in two with a flick of her tail.
Very dangerous!

Hiccup's tip: Run! No, seriously! This one's not making friends today!

There are many other dragons, about whom very little is known. With some, like the Whispering Death and the Skrill, all we know are their names. Learn those names, warrior, if you hope to survive against a dragon raid.

SCAULDRON

Sprays scalding water at its victim!

THUNDERDRUM

Produces a concussive sound that can kill a man at close range!

TIMBERJACK

Has razor-sharp wings that slice through full-grown trees!

CHANGEWING

Sprays acid at its victim!

Now its YOUR turn! Can you find all the dragons hiding in the picture?

- NIGHT FURY
☐

- GRONCKLE
☐

- DEADLY NADDER
☐

- TERRIBLE TERROR
☐

- HIDEOUS ZIPPLEBACK
☐

- MONSTROUS NIGHTMARE
☐

- BONE KNAPPER
☐

FLY YOUR DRAGON!

Riding a dragon takes a lot of practice. It also takes a few other things too – and you'll need to find them all in the grid below.

```
N A W H C G B S H I E L D
W I N G S L N I M E F O L
N I G H T M A R E D C U I
H D O H F Y M G O A L N E
I E K M T O P R Q I O G M
C P F B R F S T J G M P O
C D H H P H U P A V N D N
U G S C O M S R F L C P S
P A I L O I D M Y O H L T
O H F P W E O L G P F X E
E S M I S B F D R O W S R
Z F R A H L P G O M A T H
S A D D L E C I F R H B C
```

NIGHTFURY
SADDLE
WINGS
FISH
DRAGON
SWORD
SHIELD
HICCUP
MONSTER
NIGHTMARE
FLY
SWOOP

You should know your dragons even in the dark – just from their shapes! Can you identify the Zippleback Dragon here? Clue: it has two heads...

A   B   C

START

END

Flying a dragon takes a lot of practice! Can you find your way through the skies?

D

E

F

ANSWERS

PAGE 16
1. Dragon
2. Princess Fiona
3. Pinocchio
4. Donkey
5. Lord Farquaad
6. Shrek
7. Puss in Boots

PAGE 18
Shrek, Donkey, Princess Fiona, Puss in Boots, Dragon, Lord Farquaad, The fairy Godmother and Prince Charming

PAGE 19

PAGE 30
1. New York Zoo
2. Ten
3. A hippo
4. Four
5. Kenya Wildlife Preserve, Africa
6. King Julien
7. The foosa
8. Fish (or sushi)

PAGE 40

PAGE 41

PAGE 50
1. Po the panda
2. A goose
3. Mantis
4. Crane
5. He sells noodles
6. Nothing (there is no secret ingredient!)
7. The Dragon Scroll
8. Food (dumplings)

PAGE 55
Tigress, Monkey, Viper, Crane and Mantis

PAGE 57

PAGE 68
1. With the local blacksmith
2. Stoick the Vast
3. On the Isle of Berk
4. A Night Fury
5. Gobber (the blacksmith)
6. Six (Hiccup, Astrid, Fishlegs, Snotlout and twins Ruffnut Thorston and Tuffnut Thorston)
7. Astrid
8. Half a fish
9. A Red Death Dragon

PAGE 73

PAGE 74

C is the Zippleback Dragon

PAGE 75

DreamWorks All Stars Annual 2014

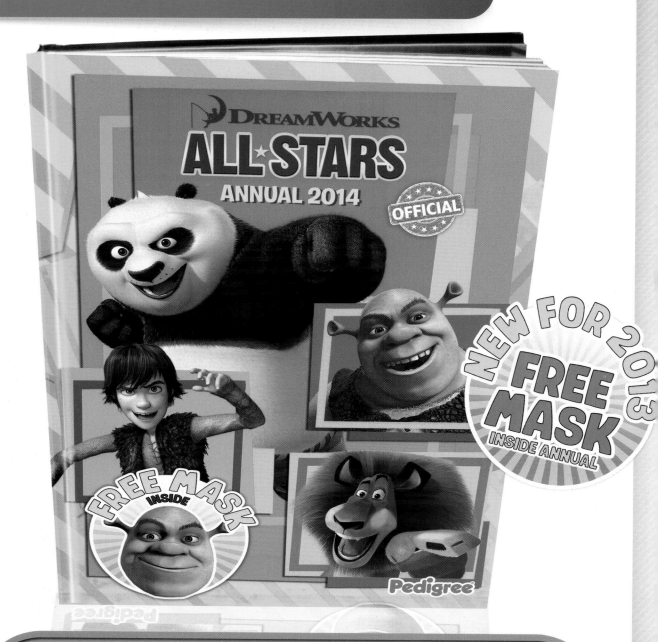

Visit **Pedigreebooks.com** to find out more on this year's **DreamWorks All Stars Annual**, scan with your mobile device to learn more.

Visit www.pedigreebooks.com

Pedigree Books, Beech Hill House, Walnut Gardens, Exeter EX4 4DH